Collector's Digest Soapstone

A Price Guide.

By L-W Book Sales.

ISBN#: 0-89538-025-0

Published by: L-W Book Sales.
P.O. Box 69
Gas City, IN. 46933

Please write for our free catalog.

Attention Collectors.....if you would like to contribute photographs or informa-tion of your collection (possibly for profit), please call L-W Books (toll free) at 1-800-777- 6450 Tuesday thru Friday 9am to 3pm.

Layout and design by Doug Kirk.
Photography by David Devon Dilley.

TABLE OF CONTENTS

Introduction

Soapstone is a material found in nature composed of magnesium silicate and other trace minerals. It is very soft and easily carved. It is also very easily stained or marred by scratches in ordinary day to day use. It may be cleaned using a light detergent or mineral spirits. The shine to soapstone may be revitalized by polishing with vegetable oil or WD-40. Be sure to polish dry.

Most soapstone items are from the Far East. The majority of the older pieces were carved in China. Some may be from Japan, India, and Thailand.

Many of the newer pieces that will be found on the market will be from India and China. Always look for wear on the feet or base of the item. Older soapstone is smooth with very few file or saw marks. Please be careful of reproductions.

Most Chinese items were made from 1890-1935. Most pieces that will be found are decorative, such as vases, bookends, match holders, toothpick holders, boxes, incense burners, etc. Soapstone was also used for utilitarian purposes, such as foot warmers, lining for heating stoves, griddles, bowls, cups, plates, saucers etc. The older and larger items are the hardest to find.

We hope you enjoy this book!

Acknowledgments

On behalf of L-W Book Sales we would like to thank the following people.
Jesse Shanks, Jonesboro, IN.
Jim Roush, Marion, IN.
Patt Dehaan, Spring Lake, MI.
Lael Boren & Melba Gibbs, Upland, IN.

Pricing Information

The coloring and intricate carvings usually demand a higher price.
Pieces with spots located at desired places also are higher.
Plain pieces naturally do not bring as much.
L-W Books and the authors accept no responsibility for profits or losses in selling or buying of Soapstone.This is only a guide.

LARGE VASES

Floral Vase Made from Two Pieces of Soapstone.
Length - 4" x Width - 2 3/4" x Height - 5"
$60+

Floral Vined Vase with Bowl & Birds.
Length - 6 1/2" x Width - 1 3/4" x Height - 8 1/2"
$85+

Floral Vined Vase.
Length - 4 1/4" x Width - 2" x Height - 6 3/4"
$65+

Large Double Vase with Floral Vine & Bird.
Length - 6 3/4" x Width - 2 1/2" x Height - 8"
$85+

Triple Vase with Floral Vine.
Length - 10 1/2" x Width - 2 3/4" x Height - 6 3/4"
$90+

Floral & Vine Vase, Length - 5 1/2" x Width - 4" x Height - 8 1/2"
$95+

Floral & Vine Vase.
Length - 5" x Width - 1 3/4" x Height - 7 3/4"
$125+

Vase on Wooden Stand, Length - 4" x Width - 3 3/4" x Height - 8"
$85+

Floral & Vine Vase.
Length - 4 1/2" x Width - 2 1/4" x Height - 10"
$140+

Vase with Oriental Man, Dragon & Other Figures.
Length - 10 1/4" x Width - 4" x Height 11 1/4"
$400+ (Circa. 1875)

Floral Vase with Birds.
Length - 9" x Width - 4 3/4" x Height - 11"
$395+ (Circa. 1875)

Floral Vine & Birds Vase withTwo Smaller Bowls.
Length 8" x Width 2" x Height 9 3/4"
$150+

Floral Vase.
Length - 4 3/4" x Width - 3" x Height - 8 1/4"
$175+

Large Floral Vase with Birds.
Length - 6 1/4" x Width - 2 3/4" x Height - 8"
$125+

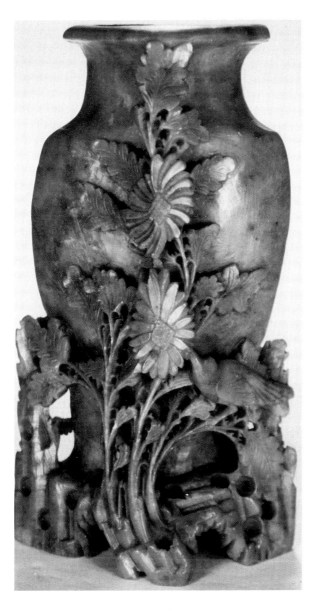

Floral and Bird Vase.
Length - 4" x Width - 2 1/2" x Height - 7"
$85+

Double Vase with Floral Vine & Bird.
Length - 6 1/4" x Width - 3 1/4" x Height - 8"
$100+

Floral Vine Vase.
Length - 4" x Width - 2" x Height - 5 1/4"
$45+

Double Vase with Floral Vine.
Length - 5 1/2" x Width - 2 1/4" x Height - 7"
$75+

Vase with Two Small Planters, Floral Vines & Birds.
Length - 8 1/2" x Width - 6" x Height - 14 1/2"
$450+ (Circa. 1880)

Floral Vine Vase Made fromTwo Pieces of
Soapstone.
Base - 2 1/4" Sq. x Height - 6"
$45+

Floral Vase & Planter with a Fish Vase at One End and a Frog on the Left Planter.
Length - 15 1/2" x Width - 3 1/2" x Height - 7"
$250+

Vine Vase.
Length - 5" x Width - 2 1/2" x Height - 7 1/2"
$75+

Floral & Vine Vase.
Length - 3" x Width - 2 3/4" x Height - 7 1/2"
$75+

Floral & Vine Vase.
Length - 5 1/4" x Width - 3" x Height - 6 1/2"
$90+

Floral Vase with Two Planters, Monkey & Bird.
Length - 6" x Width 3 1/2" x Height - 6"
$100+

Two Floral & Vine Vases.
Length - 4 1/4" x Width - 2 1/4" x Height - 6 1/2"
$75+

Floral Vase with Planter & Bird.
Length - 7 1/2" x Width - 1 3/4" x Height - 5 3/4"
$50+

Vase & Bowl with Monkeys, Birds and Squirrel.
Length - 7" x Width - 2 1/2" x Height - 8"
$185+

Floral Vases Made from Two Pieces of Soapstone.
Length - 5 1/2" x Width - 3 3/4" x Height - 5 1/2"
$120+ Pair

Floral & Vine Vase.
Length - 3 1/4" x Width - 2 1/2" x Height - 6 1/2"
$75+

Double Vase With Floral Vine.
Length - 4 3/4" x Width - 2" x Height - 5 1/4"
$95+

Floral & Vine Vase.
Length - 2 1/2" x Width - 1 1/2" x Height - 5"
$45+

Floral Vase with Match Holders & Planter, Length - 8 1/4" x Width - 3 1/2" x Height - 4 1/2"
$100+

Planter with Monkeys, Deer, Bird & Others.
Length - 8 1/4" x Width - 2 1/2" x Height - 4 1/4"
$250+

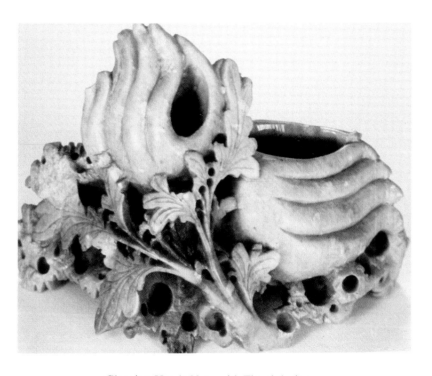

Clasping Hands Vase with Floral design.
Length - 6" x Width - 3" x Height - 4 1/2"
$120+

Double Vase with Birds & Monkey.
Length - 7" x Width - 2 1/4" x Height - 4 1/2"
$90+

Floral & Vine Vase with Bird.
Length - 4" x Width - 2 1/2" x Height - 6"
$65+

Flower Buds & Vine Vase.
Length - 3 3/4" x Width - 2 1/2" x Height - 5 1/4"
$45+

Vase with Floral Design made from two pieces of Soapstone.
Length - 4 3/4" x Width - 2 1/4" x Height - 5 1/2"
$50+

Double Vase with Floral Vine.
Length - 4 1/2" x Width - 2" x Height 5 1/2"
$60+

Double Vase with Flowers & Vine.
Length - 7" x Width - 2 1/2" x Height - 7"
$95+

Vase with Floral Vine & Bowl.
Length - 6" x Width - 2 1/2" x Height 5 1/2"
$100+

Floral Vase with Bowl and Birds.
Length - 7" x Width - 1 3/4" x Height - 5 1/4"
$145+

Vase with Floral Vine and Birds.
Length - 6 1/2" x Width - 2 1/8" x Height - 4 3/4"
$40+

Floral Vase.
Length - 5 1/2" x Width - 3 1/4" x Height - 5"
$50+

Vase with Deer, Monkey, Bat & Bird
Length - 7 1/4" x Width - 2 3/4" x Height 5 1/2"
$150+

Double Vase with Floral Vine.
Length - 4 1/2" x Width - 2 1/2" x Height - 7"
$85+

Vase with Flower Buds & Bowl.
Length - 8 1/2" x Width - 2" x Height - 7"
$150+

Vase with Floral Vine.
Length - 4 1/2" x Width - 2 1/4" x Height - 5"
$75+

SMALL VASES

Floral Vase.
Length - 5"
Width - 2 1/4"
Height - 3 3/4"
$45

Vase with Monkey &
Bird.
Length - 5 1/4"
Width - 1 3/8"
Height - 3"
$35+

Floral Vase with Bowl.
Length - 4"
Width - 2 1/4"
Height - 3 1/2"
$30+

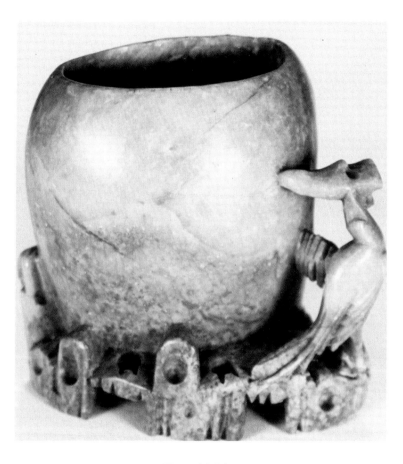

Vase with Bird.
Length - 2 3/4" x Width - 2 1/8" x Height - 3 1/4"
$40+

Double Vase with
Floral Vine.
Length - 5 1/2"
Width - 1 1/2"
Height - 3 3/4"
$40+

Double Vase with Floral Vine.
Length - 5"
Width - 1 1/4"
Height - 4"
$45+

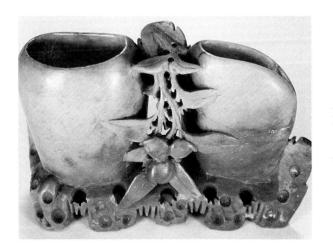

Double Vase with
Floral Vine in
middle.
Length - 5 1/2"
Width - 1 1/2"
Height - 4 1/4"
$35+

Vase with Floral Vine.
Length - 6 1/2" x Width - 2 1/2" x Height - 3 1/2"
$40+

Triple Vase with Floral Vine.
Length - 7" x Width - 3" x Height - 4"
$50+

Double Vase with Floral Vine.
Length - 5 1/4" x Width - 1 3/4" x Height - 3 3/4"
$35+

Double Vase with Floral Vine.
Length - 5" x Width - 1" x Height - 3 3/4"
$50+

Double Vase with Floral Vine.
Length - 5 1/4" x Width - 2" x Height - 4"
$25+

Vase with Floral Vine.
Length - 3 1/2" x Width - 2 1/2" x Height - 3 1/4"
$35+

Double Vase with Floral Vine.
Length - 5" x Width - 2 1/4" x Height - 3 3/4"
$50+

Pair of Floral Vine Vases.
Length - 1 3/4" x Width - 2"
Height - 5"
$75+ (Pair)

Vase with Floral Vine and
Bowl.
Length - 3 1/2" x Width - 1 1/2"
Height - 4 1/2"
$45+

Double Vase with Floral Vine.
Length - 4 1/2" x Width - 2"
Height - 4 1/4"
$45+

Vase with Floral Vine.
Length - 2 1/2" x Width - 2 1/4"
Height - 6"
$40+

Double Vase with Floral Vine.
Length - 5" x Width - 2 1/4" x Height - 4"
$40+

Vase with Floral Vine.
Length - 4 1/4" x Width -1 1/2" x Height - 4"
$50+

Double Vase with Floral Vine.
Length - 6" x Width - 2 1/2" x Height - 4"
$50+

Double Vase with Floral Vine.
Length - 6" x Width - 2 1/4" x Height - 4 1/2"
$75+

(Same as picture below but showing Bird handle, lid off.)

Small Bowl with Candle Holder.
Length - 6 1/4" x Width - 3 3/4" x Height - 4 1/4"
$125+

Small Floral Vine Vase with Bowl.
Length - 6 1/4" x Width - 2" x Height - 4"
$35+

Vase with Floral Vine.
Length - 2 1/4" x Width - 1 3/4"
Height - 3 1/2"
$25+

Vase Floral Vine.
Length - 2 1/4" x Width - 1 1/4"
Height - 3 3/4"
$25+

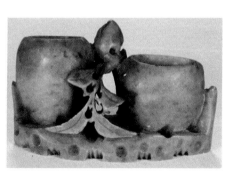

Double Vase with Floral Vine.
Length - 4" x Width - 1 1/4"
Height - 2 1/2"
$30+

Vase with eating Squirrel.
Length - 3" x Width - 1 1/2"
Height - 3 1/2"
$40+

Incense Burner Lamp.
Length - 4" x Width - 2 1/2"
Height - 1 1/2"
$75+

Floral & Leaf Bowl.
Length - 3" x Width - 2"
Height - 1 1/4"
$40+

Baby Dragon Bowl.
Length - 2 3/4" x Width - 2"
Height- 2"
$35+

Incense Burner Lamp.
Length - 3 1/2" x Width - 2 1/4"
Height - 1 1/4"
$75+

ASHTRAYS

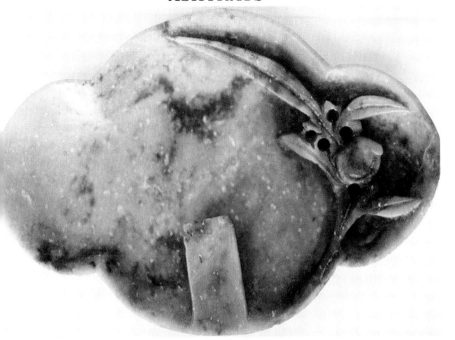

Budding Vine Ashtray.
Length - 5" x Width - 3 1/4"
$25+

Floral Vine Ashtray.
Length - 4 3/4" x Width - 3"
$25+

Ashtray with Match Holders, Length - 8" x Width - 4 1/2" x Height - 3 1/4"
$70+

Budding Vine Ashtray.
Length - 3 1/2" x Width - 5 1/2"
$25+

Budding Vine Ashtray.
Length - 4 1/4" x Width - 3 3/4"
$25+

Budding Vine Ashtray.
Length - 6" x Width - 4 1/2"
$25+

Budding Vine Ashtray.
Length - 5 1/4" x Width - 4"
$25+

Budding Vine Ashtray.
Length - 4 1/2" x Width - 3"
$25+

Tree Leaf Ashtray.
Length - 5 1/4" x Width - 4"
$40+

Floral Leaf Ashtray.
Length - 6" x Width - 3 1/4" x Height - 2 1/4"
$25+

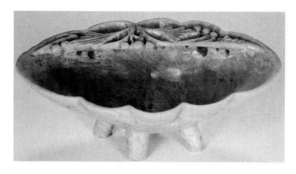

Floral Leaf Ashtray.
Length - 5" x Width - 3" x Height - 2"
$25+

Bowl & Budding Vine Ashtray.
Length - 8" x Width - 5" x Height - 4"
$75+

MATCH, STAMP & PENCIL HOLDERS

Match Holder With Bat & Bird.
Length - 5 1/2" x Width - 1 1/2" x Height - 2 3/4"
$40+

Match Holder with Leaf & Vine.
Length - 2 1/4" x Width - 1 1/4"
Height - 2 1/2"
$25+

Match Holder with Budding Vine.
Length - 5 1/2" x Width - 1 1/2" x Height - 2 1/2"
$30+

Stamp Holder with Floral Vine.
Length - 5" x Width 1 3/4" x Height - 2"
$40+

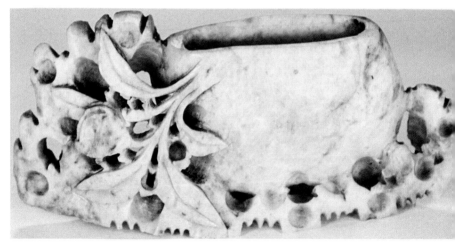

Pencil Holder with Budding Vine.
Length - 4 1/4" x Width - 1" x Height - 2"
$25+

Stamp Holder with Two Kissing Monkeys.
Length - 4 1/4" x Width - 2" x Height - 2 1/4"
$60+

Match Holder with Budding Vine.
Length - 4 3/4" x Width - 1 1/2" x Height - 3"
$35+

Match Holder with Bird.
Length - 3 1/4" x Width - 1 3/4"
Height - 2 1/4"
$25+

Match Holder with Floral Vine.
Length - 3 1/2" x Width - 1" x Height - 2 1/2"
$30+

Match Holder with Budding Vine.
Length - 5" x Width - 1 3/4" x Height - 3 1/2"
$25+

Match Holder with Budding Vine.
Length - 3" x Width - 1 1/4" x Height - 2"
$25+

Match Holder with Budding Vine.
Length - 2 3/4" x Width - 1"
Height - 2 1/2"
$20+

Match Holder with Budding Vine.
Length - 2 3/4" x Width - 3" x Height - 3 1/2"
$30+

Match Holder with Seashell &Leaves.
Length - 4 1/2" x Width - 1 1/4" x Height - 4 1/2"
(Seashell was put on at a later time.)
$20+

Match Holder with Squirrel & Monkey.
Length - 5 1/4" x Width - 1 3/4" x Height - 3 1/2"
$60+

Match Holder with Bird.
Length - 4" x Width - 1 3/4" x Height - 2"
$30+

Stamp & Pencil Holder with Floral Vine.
Length - 4" x Width - 1 3/4" x Height - 2"
$30+

Speak, Hear, and See No Evil Monkeys
Length - 4 1/2" x Width - 1" x Height - 3"
$65+

Hear, See and Speak No Evil Monkeys.
Width - 3/4" x Height - 1 3/4"
(All three Monkeys)
$10+ Each

BUDDHAS

Buddha Statue.
Length - 2 3/4" x Width - 1 1/2"
Height - 3 3/4"
$30+

Buddha Statue.
Length - 2"
Width - 1 1/2"
Height - 2 1/2"
$30+

Buddha Statue.
Length - 2 1/4" x Width - 1 1/4"
Height - 3 1/2"
$25+

Buddha Statue.
Length - 2 1/4" x Width - 1 3/4"
Height - 3 1/4"
$40+

Buddha Statue.
Length - 3 1/4" x Width - 1 1/4" x Height - 3"
$50+

ANIMALS

Trumpeting Elephant.
Length - 3" x Width - 1 1/2"
Height - 2"
$25+

Water Buffalo.
Length - 3" x Width - 1 1/4"
Height - 1 1/2"
$15+

Trumpeting Elephant.
Length - 3" x Width - 1 1/2"
Height - 2 3/4"
$20+

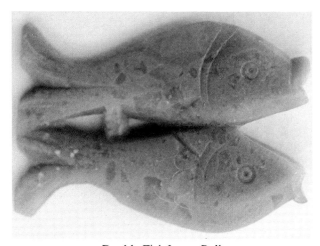

Double Fish Lamp Pull.
Length - 1 3/4" x Width - 1/8" x Height - 1 1/8"
$10+

Bird Statue & Whistle.
Height - 2 1/2"
$25+

Rooster & Hen on Top of Tree Branch.
Base - 3 1/2" Sq. x Height - 7 1/2"
$80+

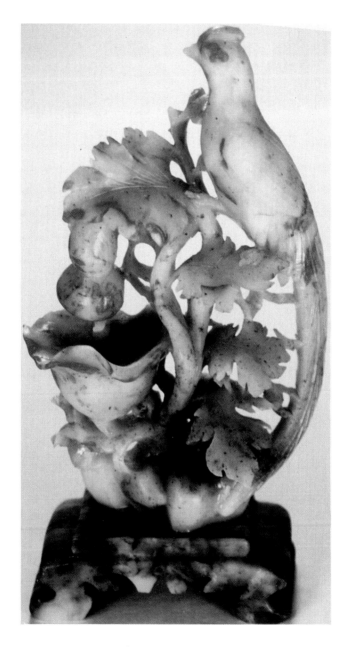

Pheasant on Floral Vine.
Length - 4" x Width - 2 1/2" x Height - 8"
$80+

Walking Crane with Tree Backgrounmd.
Length - 4 1/4" x Width - 2 1/4" x Height - 8 1/2"
$80+

TOOTHPICK HOLDERS

Toothpick Holder
with Three Birds.
Length - 1 3/4"
Width - 1 3/4"
Height - 2 1/4"
$15+

Toothpick Holder
with Monkeys &
Bird.
Length - 1 3/4"
Width - 1 1/2"
Height - 2 1/4"
$15+

Toothpick Holder with
Three Monkeys
Length - 1 3/4"
Width - 1 3/4"
Height - 3"
$35+

Toothpick Holder with Two Birds &
Two Monkeys.
Length - 3 1/4" x Width - 1 1/2"
Height - 2 1/4"
$30+

Toothpick Holder with
Three Birds.
Length - 2 1/2"
Width - 1 1/2"
Height - 2 1/2"
$15+

Toothpick Holder with Three Monkeys.
Length - 2 1/4" x Width - 2" x Height -1 3/4"
$20+

SEALS & INTRICATE CARVINGS

Wax Seal Box.
Base - 2 1/4" sq. x Height - 2 1/2"
Seal - 7/8" sq. x Height - 2 7/8"
$65+

Wax Seal Box with Seal Enclosed.

Soapstone Carving with Wax Seal on
End
1" - sq. x Height - 3 1/4"
$65+

End Piece of Wax Seal.

Wax Seal on Pedestal Base.
Seal - 7/8" Sq.x Height - 2 3/4"
$50+
(See Pedestal Base in the Reproduction Section.)

Wax Seal as Shown to the
Left
(Circa 1950)

End Piece of Wax Seal.

Stoapstone Cigarette Dispenser.
Length - 4 1/8" x Width - 1 3/4" x Height - 2 1/2"
$125+

Carving of a Pig and Piglets on a Wood Base.
Length - 6 3/4" x Width - 2 3/4" x Height - 5"
$325+

Floral Vine with Squirrels Scene.
Length - 3" x Width - 1 1/2" x Height - 3 3/4"
$20+

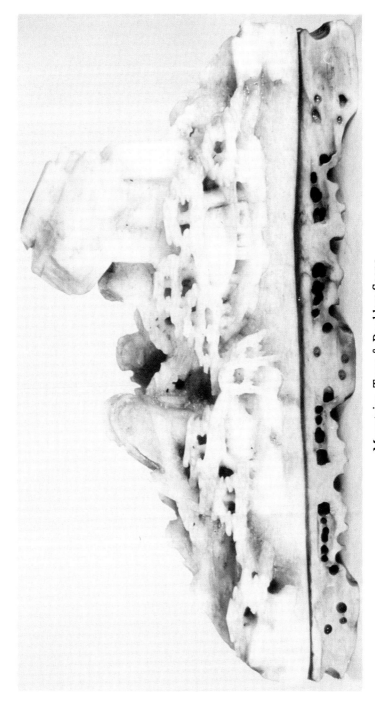

Mountains, Trees & Boulders Scene.
Length - 7 1/2" x Width - 1 3/4" x Height - 4 1/4"
$45+

Man Sitting on Rock Scene.
Length - 5" x Width - 2" x Height - 2 1/2"
$50+

Squirrel Eating on Vine Scene.
Length - 3" x Width - 1 1/2"
Height - 4 1/2"
$65+

Floral Vine with Climbing Animal.
Length - 5 3/4" x Width - 2" x Height - 5 1/4"
$50+

Leaves & Budding
Vine Scene.
Length - 4 1/4"
Width - 1 1/4"
Height - 3 1/4"
$45+

REPRODUCTIONS

New Bottle with Cork Top.
Width - 1 1/2" x Height - 2 1/2"
$15+

New Ring Box with Floral Vine
Painting on Top.
Length - 2 1/4" x Width - 1 3/4"
Height - 1 1/2"
$15+

New Cigarette and Match Holder.
Length - 4" x Width - 1 1/4" x Height - 3"
$20+

New Jewelery Box.
Dia. - 3 1/2" x Height - 3 3/4"
$30+

New Jewelery Case.
Dia. - 2 3/4" x Height - 3/4"
$10+

New Pedestal Base.
Length - 3 3/8" x Width - 1 1/4" x Height - 1 1/4"
$10+ (Circa 1950)

New Bowl with Lid.
Dia.- 1 1/4" x Height - 1 1/8"
$15+ (Circa 1950)

New Bowl with Lid.
Dia. - 1 3/4" x Height - 1 1/2"
$15+ (Circa 1950)

FOOT WARMERS

Foot Warmer.
Length - 11 3/4" x Width - 9 1/4" x Height - 2 1/4"
$25+

Foot Warmer.
Length - 8" x Width - 6" x Height - 2"
$20+

Foot Warmer.
Length - 10" x Width - 8" x Height - 2"
$25+

Foot Warmer.
Length - 9 3/4" x Width - 7 5/8" x Height - 2"
$25+

PRIMITIVE PIECES

Primitive Cup & Saucer Set. (Handmade)
Cup : Length - 4" x Width - 2 3/4" x Height - 2"
Saucer : Dia. - 4"
$40+

Confucius Statue.
Length - 3 1/4" x Width - 2 1/2"
Height - 9 1/4"
$150+

Buddha Statue.
Length - 3" x Width - 1 3/4" x Height - 7"
$125+

Unknown Statue.
Length - 3 3/4" x Width - 2" x Height - 8"
$50+

Confucius Statue.
Length - 2 1/2" x Width - 2"
Height - 5"
$40+

Lady Statue.
Length - 2" x Width - 2 1/4"
Height - 5 1/4"
$40+

Confucius Statue.
Length - 2 1/2" x Width - 1 1/2"
Height - 5"
$90+

Confucius Statue.
Length - 2 1/2" x Width - 1 3/4"
Height - 4 1/2"
$55+

Large Beetle on Tree Pod.
Length - 5" x Width - 1 1/2" x Height - 1 3/4"
$30+

Two Piece Lady Figural Set.
Length - 3" x Width - 3 1/4" x Height - 8"
$175+

Shrine with Loose Figure Inside.
Length - 2 3/4" x Width 1"
Height - 3 1/2"
$75+

Two Piece Figural Statue.
Length - 2" x Width - 1 1/2" x Height - 6 1/2"
$75+

Pointed Toe Shoe.
Length - 3 1/4" x Width - 1" x Height - 3/4"
$15+

WALLPOCKET

Floral Vine Wallpocket.
Width - 5 1/2" x Height - 7"
$175+

BOOKENDS

Floral Vine in Vase with Bird, Bookends.
Length - 3 3/4" x Width - 1 1/2" x Height - 5"
$75+

Two Monkeys Bookend.
Length - 4 1/4" x Width - 1 1/2"
Height - 5 1/2"
$40+

Floral Vine in Vase Bookend.
Length - 3 1/4" x Width - 1 1/4"
Height - 4 1/2"
$35+

Floral Vine in Vase Bookend.
Length - 3 3/4" x Width - 1 5/8"
Height - 5"
$40+

Floral Vine in Vase Bookend.
Length - 3 1/8" x Width - 1 1/2"
Height - 4 1/4"
$35+

Vase & Floral Vine Bookend
Length - 3 1/4" x Width - 1 1
Height - 4 1/4"
$40+

TABLE LAMPS

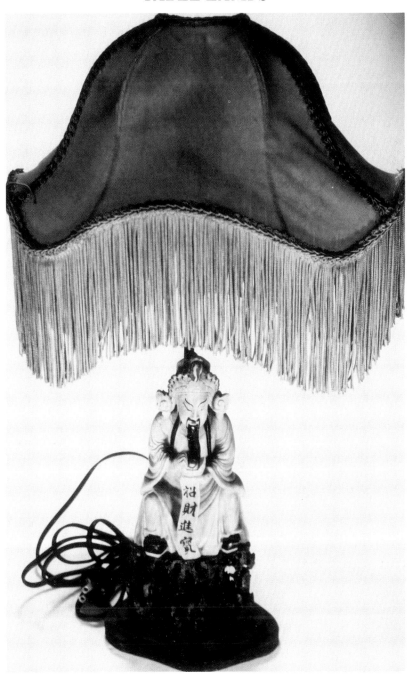

Lamp With Shade.
$500+

Lamp with Shade.
$350+